# The Success Traps

# The
# Success
# Traps

◆

## The 7 Fatal Traps
## On The Journey to Success

## Tim McMahon

Authors Choice Press
San Jose New York Lincoln Shanghai

The Success Traps
The 7 Fatal Traps On The Journey to Success

Authors Choice Press
an imprint of iUniverse.com, Inc.

For information address:
iUniverse.com, Inc.
5220 S 16th, Ste. 200
Lincoln, NE 68512
www.iuniverse.com

ISBN: 0-595-19035-9

Printed in the United States of America

As Always for Sue. Without you it would never have happened.

# Epigraph

———————— ◆ ————————

*"Success isn't about being right all the time. Mostly it's about how quickly you can figure out you're going in the wrong direction and how fast you can do something about it!"*

*"The Joy of Success is in the Journey, not the Destination."*

*"If they don't know about you then they can't buy from you."*

# *Acknowledgements*

◆

A book, just like achieving Success, isn't done in a vacuum. It relies on ideas, experiences, and feedback—and they've come from so many sources over so many years.

It always begins and ends with Sue. For 29 years of marriage she's given me unerring (if occasionally painful) advice, insight, and most of all the support and confidence I needed. More than my spouse—my very best friend in the entire world! Each book is really *her* book…

Jonathan Narducci, friend extraordinare who challenges *everything* and fuels my personal idea bank with his talent and knowledge.

My Clients whose faith and confidence have made everything possible—and who have taught me perhaps even more than I've brought them. Thank you one more time.

And good friends, just for being good friends and having good ideas—Vance Pool, Rob Mould, Jack & Linda Lockhart, Ken & Diane Asai, Pat Angulo, Bob & Meg Hamm, Chris Heide, Mike and Mary Molloy, and Linda Narducci…

And of course, the "Kids" who still aren't sure exactly what it is I do but they know it's for them—Casey, Katie, Tim, and Betsy…and Steph, our newest and favorite addition to Clan McMahon!

# Contents

# *Preface*

◆

What is Success?

It's such a great question because there's no great answer! Success, I suppose, is *what you make it!* It's whatever you decide it is. It's personal, for you, and no one else.

Success is a stretch. It's usually about accomplishing something that is important to you that makes your life better. Success can be about family or work or something very personal. It can be about your achievements in business, sport, academics, or a thousand other things. It's always about reaching a bit higher, about being the very best you can be.

*Recently an interviewer asked me, "Do you consider yourself successful?"*

*"Yes, I think so", I answered. And then I added, "But not as successful as I'm working on!"*

*"Well then," he smiled, "What advice would you give people about how they can become more successful?"*

*"Actually," I answered, "I'm not sure there's any advice I could give anyone about how to become more successful. Success is a pretty personal thing and it's different for everyone. Maybe I could tell them how to do what I've done but I'm not sure that's especially helpful."*

*"Well, what **can** you say about Success?" asked the interviewer.*

*I thought about it for a few minutes. "Achieving success is really pretty easy—if you can just avoid falling in the **Success Traps** along the way!"*

*"Really? Tell us more…"*

I've gotten most everything I've ever dreamed of and a good bit more. Some days even I'm surprised. When asked I usually attribute my good fortune to having had a lot of really good luck. But fortunately or unfortunately I have family and good friends who will correct me in front of people. *"Don't listen to him. Any "luck" he had he made!"* I suppose there's some truth in that…

I spent over twenty years in sales and management with great companies: IBM, Digital Equipment, Dun+Bradstreet, and Source Services. I did very well. Not always screamingly well but there were moments, a few flashes of brilliance, and I do have a wall full of plaques. And I learned a lot.

But that's not where the story begins. It all starts in June of 1995 on a beach…(and if you're going to start a success story, where better than a beach, I ask you?)

# *Beginnings*

◆

*Dorado Beach, Puerto Rico—*
Sue and I and the kids arrived in sunny Puerto Rico on a beautiful, hot
June day ready for two great weeks of sun, surf, and just perhaps the
occasional margarita (Sue and I, not the kids). We had a great "casita"
that opened right on to the beach under crystal clear Caribbean skies.
The perfect vacation ahead.

When I left on Friday, the president of my employer, Sales Technologies (a Dun+Bradstreet company), asked me if I would mind calling in on Monday morning.

*"I'm really sorry to ask you to do this on your vacation but we're making some important announcements that morning that I know you'll want to hear."*

*"Couldn't you just tell me now?" I asked.*

*"Sorry, can't say a thing until the official announcement! Why don't you call in after lunch?"*

Things had been going pretty well at Sales Technologies and D+B was a pretty good parent company. I suspected that we would announce expansion plans, maybe into Europe, or something similar. Whatever the announcement was going to be, I hoped it might offer some good opportunity.

Early Monday afternoon, I forced myself up from my beach lounger, picked up my margarita and headed for the telephone by the poolside bar. A half hour later I was back on the beach.

*"So, what's the big news?" asked my wife.*

*"Oh," I said, "They just wanted to announce that they were closing the company. The good news is that we get three weeks severance."*

One of Sue's greatest strengths is her practicality. *"Well, in that case, I guess we better pack up and see about getting a flight home so you can get busy and find another job."* Sue, of course, knew without looking that we had four children and less than $5,000 in the bank.

*"No, let's don't," I said." I was thinking about it on the way back to the beach (a journey of at least 3 to 4 minutes). I think we're all set. Why don't we just go in business for ourselves?"*

*"Doing what?" Sue asked.*

*"Well," I answered, "I'm not exactly sure yet but I figure we've got two weeks to figure it out…and the best part is that you're here with the president of the company! Do you want another margarita?"*

*"Two, please"*

*          *          *

There are people who have said I was very brave, that they would never have the "courage" to do what I did. There are people who have said that I was crazy (just because I had 4 kids, no cash, no customers, and no plan!). In retrospect, I tend to agree with the latter. I like to think of it as a period of extended temporary insanity and divine intervention. Consider what happened…

Shortly before we returned home I had decided on developing a sales consulting and motivational speaking business. I made a few calls to just a few friends before we left.

The day we returned home a message was waiting on the answering machine from someone at IBM. *"Tim, we wondered if you were free tomorrow to come down to New York and consult with us on a new sales offering we're considering. We can pay you $5,000 and expenses…*

A call from Apple Computer: *"Tim, would you be interested in speaking at a series of sales conferences we're planning? In addition to your speaking fee, we'd like you to have a new Powerbook laptop to use".*

A call from US West Direct: *"Tim, we're looking for a speaker for our sales conference and…"*

By Christmas, after just five months in business, we had made a *profit* of over $70,000.

Oh, did I mention that during this time of insanity and divine intervention I was working on a very simple rule of success? *If they don't know about you, they can't buy from you!*

Along with piles of faxes, hundreds of phone calls and emails, I managed to write and publish my first book, write four articles for major sales and marketing magazines, gain a publisher for a second book, and secure a contract to write a bi-weekly column for a national sales newsletter. I wanted to make sure that people noticed me!

Sounds like a lot of hard work, doesn't it? Well, absolute terror will do that to you! The truth is, however, that although it was a *lot* of *difficult* work it wasn't *hard work*—at least not in the sense of not being fun. I loved every moment of it—and still do!

By the third year annual revenues approached $300,000 and have considered to grow and grow. A recent national survey by The National Speakers Association now puts my business in the top 5—10% of all business measures including gross sales and profitability. And by the way, it's still just me in the company. Not an employee or contractor to be found. Sales, marketing, delivery, administration, web design, accounting—I do it all myself.

And we just keep on growing...

It sounds almost too good to be true, doesn't it. I feel that way myself sometimes. But it almost didn't turn out this way. There were so many times when I could have easily given up and started looking for another job.

I could have fallen into *The Success Traps*, each one of them guaranteed to trip up all my success plans and efforts. And they're sneaky—they can snag you before you even know it! Avoiding the success traps had more to do with my eventual success than anything I ever did to find business! And I still have to work to avoid them every day...

This isn't a book about how to start your own business (although if you're thinking about doing so it's not a bad place to start!). This is just a book about Success—however you define it—in sales, or in the company you work for, in sports, in your family and your friends, in your life!

If you're motivated to find your own success—and, as the golfers say, you can stay "out of the traps"—you're going to make it!

# The Success Trap #1:
## *"As God Is My Witness, I Thought Turkeys Could Fly!"*

◆

\*   \*   \*   \*   \*

**Les:** It's a helicopter, and it's coming this way. It's flying something behind it, I can't quite make it out, it's a large banner and it says, uh—Happy…Thaaaaanksss…giving!…From…W……K……R……P!!

**Les:** No parachutes yet. Can't be skydivers…I can't tell just yet what they are, but—Oh my God, Johnny, they're turkeys!! Johnny, can you get this? Oh, they're plunging to the earth right in front of our eyes! One just went through the windshield of a parked car! Oh, the humanity! The turkeys are hitting the ground like sacks of wet cement! Not since the Hindenberg tragedy has there been anything like this!

**Johnny:** Les? Are you there? Les isn't there. (composing himself) Thanks for that on-the-spot report, Les, and for those of you who just tuned in, the Pinedale Shopping Mall has just been bombed with live turkeys. Film at eleven.

**Venus:** Les! Are you okay?

**Les:** I don't know. A man and his two children tried to kill me. After the turkeys hit the pavement, the crowd kind of scattered, but some of them tried to attack *me!* I had to jam myself into a phone booth! Then Mr. Carlson had the helicopter land in the middle of the parking lot. I guess

5

he thought he could save the day by turning the rest of the turkeys loose. It gets pretty strange after that.

**Andy:** Les, c'mon now, tell us the rest.

**Les:** I really don't know how to describe it. It was like the turkeys mounted a counterattack! It was almost as if they were...***organized!!***

**Mr Carlson:** *As God is my witness, I thought turkeys could fly.*

— **WKRP in Cincinnati, Episode 8, 1978-1979**

\*        \*        \*        \*        \*

It's such a great line: *As God is my witness, I thought turkeys could fly!* In case you're wondering, turkeys—at least the Thanksgiving variety—generally can't.

It's 1978 and the first season of the new television comedy, "WKRP In Cincinnati". Some of us—especially those with a slightly offbeat sense of humor—consider the episode "Turkeys Away" as one of the great moments in TV and comedy. It's also perhaps the world's greatest example—fictional or otherwise—of a massive business "Whoops!"

If you missed it (or are simply too young to remember), then here's the story in a nutshell. For a Thanksgiving Day promotion and to stage a brilliant marketing coup over their competitors, station manager Arthur Carlson conceives the idea of dropping live turkeys over a shopping mall from a helicopter as a giveaway promotion. Sounds good. But as the turkeys plummet to the ground, crashing through car windshields and windows, the scene is described by WKRP's on-site reporter, Les Nesman, as the reincarnation of the Hindenberg disaster! When all is said and done, Arthur sums it all up with the classic phrase, "As God is my witness, I thought turkeys could fly..."

A small miscalculation. Something he just never considered. Whoops!...

Success in anything, in life or in business is a *good* thing, a positive thing! Everyone will tell you that to succeed in anything you really need to have a positive attitude and outlook. I agree; that's absolutely true. The trouble with developing a positive attitude, however, is that you can start to believe that it's *not* okay to have a *negative* attitude, that is to look at all the things that can go wrong! I call it "Positive Blindness"! And that's how "Whoops!" happens—and one of the real Success "traps".

In years of working with business people, salespeople, and entrepreneurs, I see Positive Blindness a lot. The hardest thing to ask these folks to do is to think about the reasons they might *not* be successful—what could go wrong with their plans, how their competitors might respond, what mistakes they may have made in their assumptions. Some of them can't do it or simply won't do it. It's just too painful and too scary. Almost like "if I look too hard at what can go wrong I might, God forbid, lose my positive attitude". "It might burst the bubble of my great idea—and that's no fun!"

Of course, nothing could be further from the truth. A real positive attitude, the kind that leads to real success, is one backed by confidence. Confidence comes from a combination of knowledge, experience, and having asked all the right questions, even the ones you didn't really want to hear the answers to.

When I first started my own business, I went to visit my friendly local banker for a business loan. I thought I had a great business plan, not to mention an impressively written resume that would most certainly convince any doubting soul of my future success. That's when my bubble burst.

*"What could go wrong?" asked the banker.*

*"Well, of course, I suppose there are lots of things but I feel what's important is to stay focused on the goal and be absolutely determined to achieve it", I answered.*

Banker: *"What will you do if things don't work out as you've planned?"*
Me: *"I'll do whatever takes to be successful!"*
Banker: *"And why will you be successful where others have failed?"*
Me: *"I am determined, I have great skills, and I am motivated!"*
Banker: *"What about your competition?"*

Me: *"I'm better than they are!"*
Banker: *"And if you fail?…"*
Me: *"I'll learn from my mistakes and move forward to success!"*

It was quiet for a few minutes as we sat in her office. Finally she said, "You know, that might be enough to get you hired for a job at most companies, but it's not enough for us to invest in your new business."

Obviously the woman lacked Vision…

The point? We'll call it the "Flying Turkeys Rule of Success":

***The Right Plan is the one that succeeds when every possibility, positive and negative, has been considered and prepared for. The Plan works no matter what happens!***

Success may contain "inspiration" and lots of "perspiration" but when all is said and done, it's mostly the result of "Preparation" and asking yourself the "hard questions".

Without it, that turkey just won't fly!

# *The View from My Window:*

───────────◆───────────

One of the benefits of traveling around the world is the opportunity to look for Success in different worlds and cultures—to see it expressed in many different ways by many different people.

Camera in hand, I've tried to find stories of challenge and success wherever I've gone and I've come across it sometimes in the places I least expected. This is the "View from my Window" and what I've seen while looking out...

✳      ✳      ✳      ✳      ✳

*The Thrill of Success comes when we pit ourselves against Obstacles so strong that they threaten to toss us from our safe places.*

*About the picture…*

Surfers Paradise in Queensland, Australia is home to some of the best surf and largest waves in the world. Not surprisingly swimmers are too often caught up in its powerful currents and undertows.

I watched from the beach as a team of volunteer lifeguards drove their rescue boat through line after line of breakers to reach a swimmer swept out by the strong current. With each wave, the small rubber boat strained and lifted by its bow in a white cascade of breaking water. It stood balanced upon the crest, and then suddenly dropped from view behind it. After long moments, when it seemed to me that the small boat must have capsized in the trough, it rose again to meet the next wave.

Later I asked one of the lifeguards was it dangerous going out after swimmers and surfers? I told him that I watched his boat drop from the top of each wave and that I thought it must take serious courage to ride the boat out.

The guard told me that the scary part wasn't sitting on the top of a wave, or even riding from the crest down; it was climbing back up the wall of water when you can't see or hear anything except water and wave. "For a few moments you don't know where you are. It's a bit claustrophobic. That's the test, mate!"

It occurs to me that there's a pretty good allegory for a lot of things in life. When you're on the crest, things are easy and the view of where you're going and what you're doing is pretty clear. It's when we get into one of life's "troughs" that we can lose all sense of direction and doubt that we can climb back up.

Like the man said, "That's the test, mate!"

# The Success Trap #2:
## "Be Realistic!"

◆

"He's got his head in the clouds! That boy will never amount to anything!"

They said it about Thomas Edison. They said it about Henry Ford…and the Wright Brothers…about Einstein…and about thousands of others, many of whom can be counted among the world's greatest success stories. They are the dreamers who imagined "the impossible" and somehow succeeded in making their dreams into reality.

But you say, "Edison and Einstein were geniuses, and the others probably were too!"

Maybe. And then again, maybe not. No one would argue that they were pretty bright guys but was that the root of their success? Maybe they just refused to let go of their dreams and listened to themselves, not everyone else!

When I was a young boy in the early '60's, my family moved to Denver. My Dad was the new sales manager for a small local brewery, the Tivoli Brewing Company, and occasionally he would take me to work with him. The brewery was located downtown and a bit outside the "high rent district", so on the way we would pass along Larimer Street. In those days, Larimer Street was Denver's version of skid row (today it's one of Denver's showpieces). Early in the morning, the "bums" were still sleeping curled up against barred storefronts, a few early risers panhandling the business crowd.

With the naiveté that only a 10 year old can have, I asked him "How did all those bums get that way? Didn't they go to school? Are they just lazy?"

Dad answered, "Son, there are plenty of doctors and lawyers out there. All kinds of people including some pretty smart ones. For one reason or another they decided that they just couldn't make it." He didn't tell me how they got there exactly but I did figure out that ending up on Larimer Street didn't have a lot to do with education or maybe even hard work!

My friend, Jon, made what I thought was an amazingly insightful comment about people. He said "You really can't motivate people—they pretty much have to find that inside themselves; but you *can* DE-motivate them pretty easily!"

It's a funny aspect of human nature that we are so quick to believe it when others tell us we're wrong or that we can't accomplish something—that we're not being "realistic". Most of the time it comes from people who there's little reason to think that they know what they're talking about. It doesn't matter; it's still like it came from an Oracle on High. If someone…anyone…said it, then it must be true. Our response is to immediately doubt ourselves, perhaps even toss away our dreams or ideas all because someone said it wouldn't work.

Someone once said to me that I didn't dream big *enough*! I didn't know how to handle that either!

Maybe Edison and Einstein and Ford and all the rest were successful because they didn't listen to anyone but themselves. Maybe they didn't hear it when someone said, "Wilbur, my boy, be realistic. People can't fly!"

If you don't believe it, here's an easy test. Next time you have a personal success, big or small, call up everyone you know and tell them all about it. Tell them how excited you are. Brag a little! And watch what happens.

When I started my business I had some early good fortune. In the first year I did three times more business than I thought I could. I was feeling pretty good about it and couldn't resist telling friends and business associates about how well things were going—especially the ones who had been so supportive during the beginning struggle. I really expected that they would enjoy hearing about my success. Well, some did but most didn't.

I learned that it was easy to find lots of supporters when you're down or struggling, but my "tough times" supporters either didn't want to hear about my success or felt they should caution me not to get too cocky.

And do you know what my first, gut reaction was? That's right, it was "Maybe they're right! Maybe I was just lucky!" What kept me going was listening instead to the little voice deep down that said they weren't!

Who are you listening to? Dream BIG, avoid "Being Realistic", and have faith in your dreams.

# The View from My Window:

———————— ◆ ————————

*Real Courage is putting yourself and your abilities on the line every day, win or lose, going for it all...*

*About the picture...*
London, England—

"Martin" is a street performer in London. You might find him this afternoon on Leicester Square in the West End. Each hour he marks out a space with blue tape and announces to passersby "The show will begin momentarily. Please line up on the blue tape and move up forward so everyone can see the most amazing show in London if not the entire World!"

No one has asked him to perform; no one has paid him to entertain in the park. Like us, Martin is a passerby in the park. Unlike us, he stopped to give a show.

Martin dances. He sings. His impressions are uncanny. The crowd builds, most laugh, most applaud. Some watch for a few minutes then walk away. Maybe they have somewhere to go; or maybe they don't like the show. But every hour, for 3 or 300, Martin performs again. Rain or shine; warm days and cold.

I asked Martin where he found the nerve—the courage—to perform in the middle of a park.

His answer: "Mon, it's wot I do".

"You mean this is how you earn your living? From the money when you pass the hat at the end?"

"No, mon," he said. "It's WOT I DO! I got to dance, you know? For the people. Don't matter if it's here or up some big stage."

I've started asking people, "What do you DO?" They usually answer by telling me about their job. What I really mean, however, is "What is your passion? What is it that makes you completely happy—so much so that money, prestige, or even what people think wouldn't matter?"

Most people don't know how to answer that question. Maybe they haven't thought about it or they're still looking for it. Maybe it's something that just doesn't seem practical in their busy lives. Too bad...

Martin is a very good dancer. One of these days I might see him "up some big stage". He's got talent, but more importantly he has the courage to do the thing he loves.

# The Success Trap #3:
## "Failure is A Great Learning Experience!"

◆

Don't you just love this one? "Failure is a great learning experience!" There is some truth here; you *can* learn some things when you fail. You can also *not learn anything*. There are folks who have failed, figured out what they did wrong and didn't do them again. That's good, I guess. There are also folks who failed and keep making the same mistakes over and over.

Is the implication of a "great learning experience" that everyone *should* fail? Does that mean that the smartest people are the ones who have failed over and over, and that they are now the best positioned for success (as long as they made different mistakes each time, I suppose)? No, I just think that "failure is a great learning experience" is about the only positive thing that you can say when you fail...or when you're trying to make someone feel better who has.

Let's be real. Failing stinks. Failure happens. Failing is the absolute pits. There is *nothing* worse. There is no 'feel good' way to justify it. People sometimes mess up. It's also not the end of the world, but that doesn't mean that it doesn't feel that way.

Yes, I have failed. I didn't particularly enjoy it and it cost me a lot of money. I *did* learn some things from it; mistakes that I would rather not repeat today. Looking back, however, I don't think that I could have done things differently than I did. At the time they seemed like good ideas—they weren't but they seemed that way! In other words, "Who knew?" I don't spend too much time thinking about all my mistakes. After all, there are so many that I haven't made yet still waiting for me!

Failure is just the opposite side of the coin of Success. If there is no possibility of failing then there is equally no possibility of success. In fact, you could make the case that the higher you reach for success, the farther the possible fall to failure.

So what's a person to do? Always reach low?

May I offer some alternative thoughts and strategies on Failure?

When you have failed, you must immediately endeavor to do each of the following, perhaps over and over:

- Kick yourself frequently and well—you probably deserve it.
- Blame yourself entirely unless you can absolutely prove beyond a shadow of a doubt that you had *nothing to do with it*. Do not blame anyone else.
- Experience the pain and disappointment—failing was not meant to be fun and satisfying.
- Make a list of all the stupid and wrong things you did. Read it frequently and irritate your friends with it. Hindsight is wonderful and you may as well try and learn *something* from it as long as you're here.
- Pretend you are a successful person and make fun of yourself. Be cruel! Very cruel…
- Resolve that you will never, never, never take risks again.
- Sleep curled up in your doorway with old clothes on. This will help you prepare for your eventual slide to skid row.
- Visit your friends and neighbors. Take a coffee cup with you, preferably tin, and ask them for their spare change. If you are unemployed this may not be a totally bad strategy…
- Recognize that you are wasting time doing all of the above when you could be getting on to something new and making a success of it…

# The View from My Window:

◆

*Today we can create "reality" through the lens of the camera. Sometimes knowing the difference is the greatest challenge...*

*About the picture...*
Surfers Paradise, Australia—
*I was sitting in a sidewalk café, eating lunch when the opportunity for this picture presented itself. A movie crew moved into the street and spent the afternoon filming a chase scene. Extras were enlisted from passing shoppers and diners for an afternoon's work strolling up the street as our pursued hero dodges his way through them to safety.*

It was great fun to sit back and watch the action—although the "fun" paled a bit after about the 20ᵗʰ take. No, sadly they never asked me to be an extra. I guess I didn't look Australian or something (although I can say "G'Day" with the best of them).

It's amazing how movies and television can create what appears to be reality.

✳      ✳      ✳      ✳      ✳

Traveling in Eastern Europe a few years ago, people asked me questions about America that surprised me. "Why do all Americans carry guns?" and "How many people have you shot?" were just a few of them. I realized that they had a view of life in the United States created by American television, soap operas, talk shows, and movies that was far from reality.

I tried to explain that what they saw wasn't real—it was "entertainment" (that's probably not the right word, but…). If it had been real, then there would be little reason for us to watch it. I'm not sure they were convinced.

✳      ✳      ✳      ✳      ✳

Even new technology, such as the Internet, is creating questionable realities. I heard a teacher warn her students not to rely on internet sources for a research paper. "It's not like a library," she said. "Anyone can put anything on the Web."

✳      ✳      ✳      ✳      ✳

So what is real, and what isn't? We need to constantly challenge our assumptions and even what we see and hear to assure that our Journey to Success is based upon a foundation of reality.

# The Success Trap #4:
## "Build A Better Mousetrap!"

◆

Often the route to Success is generated by a "better idea". It could be a new product...or even *you!*

I'm pretty sure that it was Ralph Waldo Emerson who said, ***"Build a better mousetrap and the world will beat a path to your door."*** Ralph was wrong...really wrong. It simply doesn't work and it has left more than a few would-be successes scratching their heads and wondering what happened.

The problem isn't with the "build a better mousetrap" section. If you've got a great idea for a new product or service or a new design or way to do something then by all means go full speed ahead with it! Maybe you have an idea for starting a new business that meets a real need—if you can just get some funding and some customers. Maybe *you* are the better mousetrap—you've worked hard and developed your skills, abilities, and performance. You deserve some recognition and reward—a promotion or salary increase. Your problem is that the world doesn't seem to be beating a "path to your door". What's wrong?

Maybe just this morning you asked yourself, "What's with those people (potential customers, the banker, your boss and co-workers, etc.)? Why can't they see a good idea when it's right in front of them?"

Let's suppose that you presented a really great idea to someone hoping for his or her encouragement, enthusiasm, or support. For some reason the light bulb just didn't go on for them. Maybe they even said, "I don't think that's such a good idea". So you're left wondering, "Why didn't they 'Get It'?"

Okay, let's see…what are the possible reasons they didn't "Get It"? By all means let's begin with the one that, being human, we're most likely to believe. They didn't "Get It" because "It's a really stupid idea!" (By the way, if they pointed out the 121 things that could go wrong with your idea or the insurmountable hurdles, that's pretty much a nice way of calling it "stupid").

In all fairness, "stupid idea" *is* always a possibility but it's actually not that likely. Your new "mousetrap" may go through a lot of changes and modifications before it becomes reality but chances are the core contains at least the beginnings of a pretty good idea. But again, being the humans that we are, you may have heard yourself uttering the phase that has no business in the vocabulary of any successful person:

*"Yeah, you're probably right…"*

I went to my town dump last weekend with a load of trash. It occurred to me that somewhere there must be a "dump" full of good ideas that got trashed because someone once called them stupid. I wish I could find it and mine it!

On the other hand, let's suppose that you refused to give up on your success idea just because you received a little negative comment. That's good. Instead you decided that your idea just needed more work and set about to perfect it. That's probably also good, unless you got stuck in *"The Search for the Perfect Mousetrap"!* You kept on working to improve and improve your "product" until it would become so perfect that no one would ever be able to criticize it. If only that were possible…either way your better mousetrap is in real danger of ending up on the trash heap.

Here are the three unassailable truths about better mousetraps and achieving Success.

First and foremost, not everybody will "Get It" no matter how hard you try, no matter how "perfect" the product. The challenge is to find the ones who probably will. In business it's called *target marketing—*

finding your customer base, the folks who are most likely to need and appreciate what you have to offer. As for the others, just block your ears.

Second, use the **20/60/20 Rule** (It's served me well!): *In any group of people, 20% will think you're a genius and really "Get It"; 60% will consider what you have to say, think about it, and some will eventually "Get It"; and finally 20% will think you're an idiot forever.* Believe it! If you're getting 20/60/20 you're doing something right!

Third, and most important, you *have to learn how to Sell!*

I have a sign above my desk that says, **"If they don't know about you they can't buy from you!"** The world will never beat a path to your door unless you tell the world that you're there and how much you have to offer.

Bob is an engineer by training and years of experience. Last year Bob decided to go into business for himself as a consultant. He's developed an innovative software design process and toolset that software engineering firms should be knocking down his door for. But Bob still doesn't have any business and is about to give up.

"Bob", I said, "You've got to learn how to *sell* yourself, your products and your services. Get on the phone, make sales calls on companies and engineering people that you think you can sell to. Put together a powerful 'selling' website and a brochure. You've got to let people know that you've got a real winner to offer them! Remember what I said, 'If they don't know about you…'".

So what do you think Bob's response was?

"SELL????" cried Bob. "*I am NOT a salesman! I'm an engineer. Besides if what I have is good it should be clearly obvious.*"

I suspect that Bob believes that "selling" is the task of getting people to do something or buy something that they wouldn't have otherwise. So having to *sell* his product is demeaning—and even suggests that he and his product have no real value!

Granted that in some circles Sales, unfairly I might add, might not be considered the most lustrous of professions, especially if it's defined that way. So let's try on a new definition of selling:

*"SELLING" is the task of communicating with people to make SURE that your potential customer or audience absolutely, positively 'Get's It'"!*

In other words, you just can't assume that what is obvious to you is obvious to someone else. If they figure it out on their own that's great, but by and large, it doesn't happen. It doesn't matter whether what you have to sell is yourself (for that raise or promotion), a product/service that you're offering, an idea that you want others to believe in, or an action you want someone to take. *Selling* is showing them *WHY* you believe in yourself, your idea, or your product—and what it can do for them!

Great salespeople can be found in all walks of life. Successful teachers, ministers, executives, and leaders of all kinds (and of course Salespeople). They actively "sell" their ideas—their "products"—every day. Was Martin Luther King a great salesperson? How about Microsoft's Bill Gates? You bet!

In a journey to success, doing great things and waiting for the world to notice has never worked and never will.

The journey to Success only starts with a better mousetrap. It is the *continuous* selling that brings people down the path to your door! That's right, continuous! You've got to sell every single day if you want results!

Absolute truth!

# The View from My Window:

———————◆———————

*Each of us is the Sole & Final Navigator of our Journey to find Success…*

*About the picture—*
*Boston Harbor, Massachusetts*
In the days of the great clipper ships, the success of a voyage was measured by the time it took a vessel to sail between far ports to deliver and

sell its cargo. Among competing ships, it was the skill of the Navigator that ultimately spelled success or failure for the shippers, the Captain, and the crew.

The Navigator planned his course and was constantly vigilant in case his ship was pulled off course by winds, storms, or ocean currents. A skilled navigator who could not only plan the best course but also make sure it was unerringly followed was the most important ingredient of Success.

We each embark upon many journeys for success in life. How well do we plan our course? How well do we track and measure our progress and direction? Are we the Navigators of our future or just being pushed along by any current and tide?

Even the best, fastest, most powerful ship will be lost without a Navigator who knows the way…

# The Success Trap #5:
## "Be Smarter Than The Average Bear!"

◆

*Assumption: Successful people are smart.*
*Assumption: The most successful people are the smartest!*
*Conclusion: It's important to act like you're confident and really smart if you want to be seen as successful.*
*Conclusion: Don't let anyone see you sweat!*
*"Smarter than the Av-er-age Bear!"—Yogi Bear*

          *            *            *

In the mid-1970's and early 1980's I worked for Digital Equipment Corporation, at that time second only to IBM in the computer industry. Although DEC became part of Compaq Computer a few years ago, many of us who worked there in those years have fond memories of the company in its heyday. Few companies were better to work for or fostered greater creativity and independent thinking in their employees! All in all, a great place to work and to learn.

I had just come from a field sales position into corporate headquarters as a new sales training manager, and worked in a division headed by Stan Olsen, one of DEC's two founders. Ken and Stan Olsen conceived and started DEC. Ken became President and CEO and Stan a Senior Vice President.

Now, Ken Olsen was a dynamic and forceful leader. A powerful motivator. He seemed to always know what he wanted and how to achieve it.

He was bigger than life; the man who was leading all of us to success. Frankly, everyone was pretty much in awe of Ken.

Stan was different. An engineer by profession, I remember Stan as quieter, a listener—a man who considered everything carefully before he made a decision. Stan didn't always seem to have a lot to say but he asked a lot of questions. "What are you doing? Why are you doing it this way?" When I once told Stan about a problem we were dealing with, I was amazed when he asked *me*, "What do you think we should do?"

Who was the smarter, the more successful of the Olsen brothers? That's a patently unfair question. Still, as much as I admired Ken (and still do), I always gave the edge to Stan. Ken was clearly the visionary and the leader but Stan did one thing that I felt made him stand above: *he surrounded himself with brilliance.*

Stan Olsen didn't *have* to be brilliant in his own right (although he certainly was). His real brilliance was in how he developed a team of incredibly talented and brilliant Vice Presidents and continuously "mined" their intelligence and ideas. Stan and his VP's pioneered new products, opened new markets, and designed new concepts for DEC that in many respects set the tone for the technology marketplace of today. And last I heard, each of his VP's went on to outstanding careers of his own.

Being successful—in life or in business—is too often confused with personal *brilliance*. Success it seems goes to the smartest, the hardest working, the "leaders", the movers and the shakers, the ones with all the answers. "If you want people to see you as a success, act confident—never let them know you don't have all the answers!"

Well, I don't know about you, but if experience has taught me anything it's that I have very few of the answers! I wish I had them all but, plain and simple, I don't—and obviously I'm willing to admit it! I do have lots and lots of ideas but I've also proven that more of them are clunkers than diamonds! I should also mention that I'm not all that good at acting like I have all the answers either (my wife sees through me on a regular basis).

What I am pretty good at, though, is *Mining*. I look for advice, opinion, and ideas everywhere. I find them in the newspaper and magazines, in overheard conversations on airplanes and restaurants, from my competitors, from my friends, from partnerships and alliances I've developed, from my customers—and, of course from my wife and family! The thing is, I probably disagree with what I hear far more than I agree, but that's okay. It's the continual input of ideas that let's me *learn* and makes me *think*, that helps me create my own ideas and success strategies (the ones that work!), and test them to see if they'll actually fly.

When I first started my own business, I began an *Idea Bank*. An Idea Bank was a place that I would record every good idea I came across—mine or anyone else's. The account will never be full but it's become so packed with ideas that it's paying dividends on a regular basis.

What's the bottom line? You don't have to be brilliant to be successful. You don't have to be smarter than everyone else to be the *most* successful. You do have to be willing to *learn* and to *think*, however.

Oh by the way, never tell anyone that you listened to anyone else or got an idea from anywhere except your own head. After all, it's important to maintain that "I'm smarter that the average bear" image!

# *The View from My Window:*

◆

*The true measure of Partnership is in how we help each other over Life's little obstacles...*

*About the picture...*
Versailles, France—
I was looking out my hotel room window when I saw this French couple preparing to cross the street. I was taken with the way they held each other's hand as they prepared to negotiate the curb—he taking her bag as he stepped off first to help her down.

I thought about their partnership, imagining it to be the product of long years together—all expressed in helping each other over one of life's little obstacles.

\*          \*          \*          \*          \*

I've observed that children naturally compete with each other to see who's the fastest, the strongest, or the bravest. For a child, winning is not about achieving a goal; it's about victory over his or her peers.

As adults it's often not so different. As we strive for business and personal success, we can become singularly focused on "victory"—defeating our competitors, sometimes our co-workers, and even the resistant customer. In this single-mindedness, we can lose focus on one of our most powerful success tools—partnership. Often talked about, rarely well executed.

Real partnerships are based on values, not products or politics. They take time to create, effort to maintain. Their currency is trust; their measure mutual success. Partnerships only work when each partner makes sure the other crosses the street safely…

Perhaps it's the measure of maturity and adulthood when the achievement of results becomes more important than victory…and the quest for "partnership" replaces the need for "dominance".

# The Success Trap #6:
## "No One Said It Was Supposed to Be Fun!"

◆

Why not? Why shouldn't the journey to success be incredibly fun all the time? Who said you have to work hard to be successful? Is there a connection between *fun* and *success*?

We're getting into some tricky territory here. This trap sounds like some serious heresy! Can you *not* work hard and still be successful, short of winning the lottery?

Did you ever notice the guy at work who is always the first to arrive in the morning and the last to leave? Everybody always says, *"Man, that Jack really puts the hours in!"* If you've noticed "Jack" then you may have noticed that he's not necessarily the most successful person in the company. Hard work doesn't guarantee success.

Who *is* the most successful and what do people say about *them*?

*"He/She's really good and makes it look so easy!"*

Those *successful people* always look like they're having *fun.* You would think they would look exhausted but instead they seem to be filled with energy and enthusiasm. Strange…

*"Well, success will do that for you!"*

I wonder if successful people were serious and exhausted before they were successful? Were they then magically transformed? Did *fun* just appear once they had "made it"?

*"Who ever said that work (or Life) was supposed to be Fun?"*

It's odd, but almost every really successful person I have ever known says that they actually had *more fun* on the way to Success than once they actually reached their goals. Makes you wonder if having fun has something to do with achieving success.

A college student told me that he was a majoring in business and planning to go on for an MBA. I said, "That's great. You must really enjoy Business!" He answered, "Not really. I'd rather do something else but Business is where the money is. I'll enjoy the money!"

If the most successful people found more enjoyment "in the journey than the destination" then maybe the college student has the cart before the horse because I expect he's not going to enjoy the trip.

My daughter asked me what I thought she should do in life. What should she major it, what career should she pursue. I said, "Figure out what you like to do more than anything else—the absolute most fun thing you can think of—and go for that!" She thought for a while and told me that she loved doing illustrations and artwork.

*"But, Dad, who would want to hire me for that? It doesn't seem like I could make a lot of money either."*

*"Try thinking of it this way," I said. "If you're really having fun doing something, the chances are that you will become exceptionally good at it. If you're really good, success…and money…will take care of themselves."*

Consider the converse: people who are not doing something that they really love or do well at tend to find very little "fun" in it. They rarely, if ever, become real "top performers" with the success/money it brings. And for those who "gut it out" and actually do get to the top, they may too often find they don't enjoy their success nearly as much as they thought they would (if the journey didn't kill them first).

"Dan" was determined to get to the top of IBM. He and his wife often spoke about how you "have to make some sacrifices along the way" if you're going to make it. Together they endured relocations and uprooting of their family every couple of years, good and not-so-good assignments, long days and nights, and company politics. But "Dan" progressed steadily ahead one promotion after another.

"Dan" never made to the top of IBM although he came very close. In the end, he was just in the wrong position at the wrong time when a corporate restructuring eliminated his position. Not his fault really—a miscalculation. Just one of those things that happens. Shortly thereafter, a new opportunity opened for Dan outside of IBM, one that brought him even more success than he had planned for. "Still," his friends said, "you must have been crushed when IBM fell through for you after all your hard work." "What hard work?" answered Dan. "We had a great time and besides everything worked out—just not exactly the way we planned!"

Just so there's no confusion, real work will always be a component of success. When the work is *fun*, however, I question the use of the word *hard*. I work a great deal and I have put a lot of effort into making my life and my business a success. But did I work "hard"? I know that it's a matter of semantics, but to me "hard" implies doing work that you don't really enjoy—and I certainly have not had much of that!

**If you're not having Fun, maybe you're working too hard!!**

# The View from My Window:

———————— ◆ ————————

*Listen to the Sound of your own Beautiful Music...*

*About the picture...*
London, England (Leicester Square)—
I had to get a picture of this man. I saw him sitting by the entrance to the London Underground, happily playing his bongo drum as the crowds passed by. Occasionally someone would throw a coin in the brass bowl at his feet.

I moved around, unobtrusively I hoped, to try and get a good angle for the picture. Some of the best photographs happen when no one really notices you or your camera. But just as I prepared to hit the shutter, he looked at me. Instead, however, of giving me a startled look or turning away, he just closed his eyes. He leaned his head back and then smiled a smile of pure contentment and joy as he played…

I don't know anything about him but I believe he heard the sounds of his own beautiful music…a kind of success on his own terms!

# The Success Trap #7:
## "Success Is A New Mercedes!"
◆

Everyone defines success on his or her own terms—and that's about the only way you will ever find it. When you define it on someone else's terms or expectations it becomes elusive at best, unsatisfying at its worst.

What does "the world" say success is? The big house with a new Mercedes in the driveway? A big bank account? Recognition and status? Beauty, fame, security, happiness? Holding a top company position?

It's not what the world says that matters. Success can be *anything* you want it to be. It is whatever *you* define it to be. It's what works for you and only you! Success should be whatever makes you incredibly happy and that you're willing to strive for. The problems arise when we confuse what we think we really want with what we're told we *should* want.

We've all heard the stories of "successful" people who, after accumulating riches and power, were still not happy. (I personally have often wept for them contemplating the depths of their misery.) I have to think that the only possible explanation is that what they achieved wasn't actually "success"! It looked liked success, it walked like success, but once they got it, it wasn't what they really wanted.

So it's confusing…*what do I really want from life?* There are so many mixed messages. It seems like everyone is telling you what you should want or what you should aspire to. How on earth do you figure out what's right for you?

It's especially easy to confuse success with accumulating *things* (like a new Mercedes). Success really doesn't have a lot to do with things. It's much more about achieving a certain quality of life that makes you happy—which could, of course, include having lots and lots of really great things! But it doesn't have to.

When you really get down to it, success for most people is ultimately about achieving and perfecting one or more of *The Four Life Values…Power, Fame, Relationships, or Safety.*

## *The Four Life Values*

**Power—**

Power is all about *Control, Achievement, and Status.* "Power People" achieve success when they can gain more control of the world around them and their position in it. It may be having control of their own lives and destinies; it may be gaining "positional control" as a leader or manager in a corporate or organizational setting. Control is important because it enables them to aggressively move to achieve whatever objectives they may have. Equally as important as achieving goals, is status and recognition. "Power" wants to be tangibly and publicly recognized for what he or she achieves and measured against others. So money, corporate position, home, auto, or other "trappings" of power can be important visible measures of success.

"Power" is also a planner and a decision maker. He or she will take moderate, considered risks when confident that all necessary information has been gathered and that all outcomes and options have been considered. "Power's" goals then are aggressive, but equally realistic and achievable.

**Fame—**

For "Fame", success is all about *Applause.* "Fame People" live for *Achievement, Recognition* and the *Approval* of those around them— their audience. "Fame" dreams the great dreams, and may set lofty one-chance-in-a-million goals. "Fame" is accused of *flying by the seat of the pants* because he or she often resists details and planning and prefers to make decisions on intuition, creative ideas, and feelings. "Fame" is a great risk-taker believing that only great risks can bring great rewards. The strong possibility of failure always exists but "Fame" stays focused on the dream.

Fame is an on-stage, "Star" personality because achievement without recognition is not really success. The physical trappings of success may be unimportant. What is important, however, is the immediate response and positive feedback of those around them.

"Fame" may be an entrepreneur in business. He or she loves the unstructured, creative, high-risk environment of a start-up. Unpredictability and change are positives, not negatives because they challenge "Fame's" ability to overcome unanticipated obstacles. For exactly these reasons "Fame" may not be as successful in a structured corporate environment.

Relationships—

"Relationship People" value exactly that: their *Relationships* with *People*. Mutual positive *Feelings* are most important as well as the give and take of thoughts, ideas, concerns, and emotions. Honesty, caring, and openness are highly valued as well as the importance of family.

"Relationship" is a *caregiver* and may often put other's feelings or needs above his or her own. Decisions should be made by consensus; confrontation should be avoided unless there is no other option. Success is measured by the strengths of the relationships he or she builds and maintains. Relationship" will take moderate risks but only when he is confident that a decision or action is beneficial to others.

"Relationship" people are often drawn to human-service professions that value their strong abilities for one-on-one interaction and focus upon feelings and interpersonal relationships.

**Safety—**

"Safety People" generally value *Predictability* and *Security* above all else. "Safety" likes to deal with facts and values orderly processes, "Safety" is generally risk-averse unless he or she is convinced of a compelling reason or that all possible outcomes have been fully considered and prepared for.

Not surprisingly, "Safety" people may often be drawn to positions and careers that are process driven and utilize facts and figures to generate highly predictable results. Engineering, information technology, finance and accounting—all reflect "Safety's attention to detail and data.

Just as "Fame" can be blindly optimistic, "Safety" runs the risk of pessimism and the assumption that the "glass is always half-empty". "Safety" may view Success as the reduction of risk and maintenance of the status quo.

*        *        *        *        *

Most people have a mix of these Life Values and have a broader mix of success goals. For example, "Fame" may be focused on achieving stardom but not at the expense of his or her family and friends. What we do know is that each of us ultimately determines our personal definition of Success from our unique mix of Life Goals—unless we make the mistake of letting others define it for us.

Take a look again at the Four Life Values. "Power" and "Relationship" are in many respects opposites, as are "Fame" and "Safety". Neither is good or bad but they value vastly different things. Perhaps you value spending time with family and friends as success (Relationships) but you're being told that you should be spending more time at work to get ahead in the company (Power). So who is "whispering in your ear" and telling you how you should define success? It doesn't matter if it's your spouse, your parents, your boss, or a well-meaning friend. What they're telling you is colored by their Life Values, not necessarily yours! It's one case where opposites do not attract!

In other words, "Consider the Source!"

*Success is not always a new Mercedes!*

# The View from My Window:

————————◆————————

*A Sad Face is only Funny on a Clown...*

*About the picture...*
Las Vegas, Nevada—
One of the world's most famous circus clowns was Emmet Kelly of
The Ringling Bros. Barnum & Bailey Circus. Emmet was the original
"Sad Clown".

Emmet would walk around the ring, sweeping up with his broom, with a look of world-weary sadness. Audiences loved it. Imagine! A Sad Clown! How funny!

Too bad it doesn't work that way in the real world.

In the real world, we value people with strong positive attitudes and an upbeat outlook on life—people who smile, who have a bearing about them that says "Life can be good, all challenges can be met, all obstacles surmounted!"

These are the people we want in our lives, that we choose as our friends and our leaders.

We consider them a success. As for sad people? Well…at least sometimes they're funny.

# Am I On Track for Success?

◆

Okay, let's suppose that you now have a pretty good idea of what you want from life and your personal path to Success. Here are a few final thoughts…a short personal "test" to see if your Success Goal is really right for you and if you're on track today.

- What do you really want? Power, Fame, Relationship, or Safety or some mix of these? Will the Success Goal that you have set for yourself give you what you really need? Did you set the goal or did you listen to "other voices"?
- Will getting there be is as much fun as being there? We're back to that *fun* thing again but it's really the key to everything. If you're not having fun then why are you doing it?
- Will it take hard work to achieve? It might be *lots* of *difficult* work, but it shouldn't be *hard work.*
- Will it pass the "Stupid Idea" test? Do you believe in yourself and what you want enough that you can weather the "nay Sayers"
- Can you stay on track when your idea of success doesn't match other people's—or what others tell you it *should* be?
- Can you create a Plan, a step-by-step action plan that will get you where you want to go?
- Do you know how you'll keep going even when your plan doesn't work out exactly the way you thought it would? Can you "blow off" *failure* as just a minor setback—and still keep going?

- Are you willing to listen and learn, use every possible resource? Have the humility to know that no one, least of all you, has all the answers?
- Are you ready to *SELL* the entire world if necessary to gain the Success you want?

*Then go for it!...*

# The View from My Window:

———————— ◆ ————————

Boston, Massachusetts—

**Success is not being right all the time... no one ever is. The measure is knowing if you're on the right track... and how quick you can do something about it if you're not!**

Boston Sunset - August 2000

# The Idea Bank—and How to Find Great Ideas for Success!

―――――――――――――― ◆ ――――――――――――――

Success is never achieved in a vacuum. If we take the time to look and listen we come across great success ideas every day. Ideas that motivate…or solve a problem…or open a new opportunity for success. Thoughts for my personal "Idea Bank" have come from every imaginable source—books and newspapers, television, great speakers, business associates, friends and family. Occasionally they even come from me! An idea occurs to me at night, while waiting for an airplane or driving in the car.

Sometimes great ideas are just what you need right then. More often they're an idea that you want to keep for future reference…maybe a motivational thought that you would like to keep in mind.

I used to write all these great ideas I came across on scraps of paper or on the backs of business cards. Not too surprisingly I promptly lost most of them. Actually they're probably still hidden deep in one of my desk drawers but that's the "black hole of Calcutta"—once in and never to be seen again (and rumored to be the home of small furry creatures)! Hence the Idea Bank…a simple place to store and find your wealth of Great and even not-so-great Ideas. You'll find a simple but effective Idea Bank to get you started in the Appendix of this book.

I do have a lot of ideas. As I've said, there are a lot of clunkers but fortunately a few great ones that have really paid off. Again, you just can't have too many ideas. Even the clunkers can teach you something. When

I need a good idea (and that's most of the time!) I've always found that the best approach is to go for volume and then mine through them looking for a good one. Of course it helps if you've got a lot of ideas to begin with.

My friend and business associate, Jonathan Narducci, once asked me, *"Where do you get all of your ideas? Every time we talk you come up with some new ideas to get new business or for a new program!"*

*"That's easy,"* I answered. *"From you."*

*"Me?"*

*"Sure,"* I said. *"I listen to what you say, then I think about it, add some of my own thoughts, and Voila! A New Idea!"* (Remember, I never said they were all *great* ideas!)

*"Do I get paid for my contribution?"* asked Jon.

*"No."*

### Create an Idea Factory

Do you want to generate some great ideas of your own? Do a little creative thinking? Then create an *Idea Factory*.

Think of it as a manufacturing process. You have to begin with *Raw Materials*. So get started by collecting lots of thoughts and ideas in your personal *idea bank*. You can't have too much raw material! The more you have, the greater your capability to produce something great.

Now move to the Preparation step. Think about the challenges you face and what you're trying to achieve. Read through your idea bank. Don't look to find an exact solution there (although it's fine if you do!) but just browse to remember what's inside and to fill up your *idea hopper*.

Now it's time to start the *Processing* step. This is the tricky part because there's nothing you can really do that will start ideas immediately spewing out. Creative thinking is mostly a function of the subconscious mind. The subconscious works pretty much autonomously—pose a problem to it, fill it with enough raw materials, sit back and let it work. It does work and it will if you give it a chance.

We're not done yet! We still have the *Output Process* ahead. Believe it or not, your subconscious is working and ideas are starting to flow—but you'll miss them unless you *take* time and *make* time to *Listen!*

I make "idea time" for myself almost every morning. The kids leave for school at 7:30AM and the house (and my home office) are quiet. 7:30 to 8:30 is my idea time. I sit down with a cup of coffee and a notepad, turn on "Good Morning America" and spend an hour or so *listening to myself and thinking.* If you wonder about the *GMA* thing, notice that I didn't say this was like transcendental meditation—absolute quiet not required. I think about the day ahead, the projects I'm working on, review my "to do's" and pose problems to myself—*How could I do this better? Where could I find some new business? Is there another way to do this that's more efficient and effective?* Then I listen to myself—and write down whatever comes to me. Sometimes there's a gold mine of ideas and sometimes not much at all. That's okay; ideas come at their own speed—maybe I need to put a little more in the "idea hopper" to increase production!

*Idea Time* for you might be on the way to work, in the evening before bed, or any other time that you can at least be by yourself. Many of my best ideas pop up during a solo lunch or dinner when I'm traveling. On an airplane works pretty well for me too or in a hotel room during a business trip. Whatever works for you.

Give it a try using The Idea Bank worksheets in the back—and carry them with you. You never know when you'll come across a really good idea!

# *The View from My Window:*

◆

## We learn more by watching and listening than by doing ...

*About the picture—*

Sopron, Hungary

Sopron is a beautiful medieval town in Hungary, not far from Vienna, Austria. On a summer Sunday morning I walked along the cobbled streets of Sopron, toured ancient churches, climbed a tower, sampled a glass of fine local wine in a quiet sidewalk café. As I toured I passed a certain house several times, notable only because of the couple leaning out of the window just watching people go by.

They stood there for hours, sometimes quietly talking to each other but mostly just watching. I have no idea if they observed anything profound or even especially interesting but they seemed to be enjoying themselves. I wondered when was the last time that I just took the time to watch the world go by…and what I might learn if I did.

In our search for Success, we're mostly "Do-ers". We all want to be proactive and busy making things happen; driving for achievement. Sometimes, however, we might learn as much or more from taking some time to just watch and listen.

# Afterword
# Final Thoughts

───────── ◆ ─────────

Years ago during a job interview, my future sales manager Roger asked me *"What is your goal five years from now?"*

*"I have no idea",* I answered.

*"I've never had anyone give me that answer before,"* said Roger. *"You seem motivated so I can't understand why you wouldn't have any goals for yourself. Frankly, it worries me!"*

*"To tell you the truth,"* I said, *"I have lots of goals but you asked me what they would be in five years. I could tell you that I want to be in sales management or that I want your job and that would sound great right now. But in five years I might want something completely different."*

*"So what is your plan for Success?"* he asked.

*"Actually it's pretty simple. I'm focusing on today– on being a top performer right now. I figure that if I do that and continue to do that, then there will be no shortage of opportunities for me in five years!"*

Roger still wasn't too crazy about my answer but I did get the job. Roger never did figure out exactly what to do with me, however.

\*      \*      \*      \*      \*

Abraham Lincoln is credited with the statement, *"I shall study and make ready and someday my chance will come."* I first read those words in 5th grade and they've stuck with me ever since. Abraham Lincoln was an Opportunist!

\*      \*      \*      \*      \*

The journey to Success is made up of so many things, not least of which are Preparation, Attitude, and Effort. It is also watching for *Opportunities for Success* and taking advantage of them when they come!

*　　　*　　　*　　　*　　　*

"Success" is a result. It's where we are once the goal has been achieved. But this book has been about the Journey—about the getting there. The "Journey to Success" isn't a tangible thing really; it's a state of mind, an attitude made up of hope, incurable optimism, persistence, a willingness to make the necessary effort, a commitment to personal excellence, and (most of all) an unshakeable belief that everything is going to turn out well.

**The Journey is about listening to your own inner voice, following your own intuition, and learning everything you can along the way. It is a state of mind…**

My personal definition of success today is different than when I was 23. I've learned things, raised a family, been exposed to more choices and possibilities, and my priorities have changed in so many ways. That has been a continuous process throughout my career. Fortunately I recognized this pretty early on and decided that success for me was going to be about always having options—enough options that I could go most any way I wanted in the future. So I developed my **Simple Three-Point Plan** for Success:

1. Excel at whatever I am doing at the moment, learn everything I can from every experience, and take some time to *Think*.
2. Keep my eyes always open for new opportunities
3. Believe in myself and trust my intuition

If I have learned anything in my personal journey (which isn't anywhere near over, by the way), it's this—and it may prove frustrating to some folks:

### *Success doesn't necessarily come when you want it to!*

Over the course of my career to date I've had many *successes* but it's only in the last six or seven years that I found my *Success*. All the years before have turned out to be my learning time. The experiences I had, the lessons I learned, and the effort I put forth were what prepared me for today. I didn't really know it at the time but that's how it worked out. So I was ready to grab for the brass ring when it passed by…

I'm still listening to Mr. Lincoln. I continue to study and make ready—and above all, watch for my chances!
—Tim McMahon, June, 2001

# Appendix
# The Idea Bank

◆

| Date: |
|-------|
| Source: |
| Idea: |
| |
| |
| |
| |
| |

| Date: |
|-------|
| Source: |
| Idea: |
| |
| |
| |
| |
| |

| Date: |
| Source: |
| Idea: |
| |
| |
| |
| |
| |

| Date: |
| Source: |
| Idea: |
| |
| |
| |
| |
| |

| Date: |
| Source: |
| Idea: |
| |
| |
| |
| |
| |

| Date: |
| Source: |
| Idea: |
| |
| |
| |
| |
| |

| Date: |
| Source: |
| Idea: |
| |
| |
| |
| |
| |

| Date: |
| Source: |
| Idea: |
| |
| |
| |
| |
| |

| Date: |
| Source: |
| Idea: |
| |
| |
| |
| |
| |

| Date: |
| Source: |
| Idea: |
| |
| |
| |
| |
| |

| Date: |
| Source: |
| Idea: |
| |
| |
| |
| |
| |

| Date: |
| --- |
| Source: |
| Idea: |
| |
| |
| |
| |
| |

| Date: |
| --- |
| Source: |
| Idea: |
| |
| |
| |
| |
| |

| Date: |
| --- |
| Source: |
| Idea: |
| |
| |
| |
| |
| |

| Date: |
| --- |
| Source: |
| Idea: |
|  |
|  |
|  |
|  |
|  |

| Date: |
| --- |
| Source: |
| Idea: |
|  |
|  |
|  |
|  |
|  |

| Date: |
| --- |
| Source: |
| Idea: |
|  |
|  |
|  |
|  |
|  |

| Date: |
| --- |
| Source: |
| Idea: |
| |
| |
| |
| |
| |

| Date: |
| --- |
| Source: |
| Idea: |
| |
| |
| |
| |
| |

| Date: |
| --- |
| Source: |
| Idea: |
| |
| |
| |
| |
| |

| Date: |
|---|
| Source: |
| Idea: |
| |
| |
| |
| |
| |

| Date: |
|---|
| Source: |
| Idea: |
| |
| |
| |
| |
| |

| Date: |
|---|
| Source: |
| Idea: |
| |
| |
| |
| |
| |

| Date: |
|-------|
| Source: |
| Idea: |
| |
| |
| |
| |
| |

| Date: |
|-------|
| Source: |
| Idea: |
| |
| |
| |
| |
| |

| Date: |
|-------|
| Source: |
| Idea: |
| |
| |
| |
| |
| |

| Date: |
| --- |
| Source: |
| Idea: |
| |
| |
| |
| |
| |

| Date: |
| --- |
| Source: |
| Idea: |
| |
| |
| |
| |
| |

| Date: |
| --- |
| Source: |
| Idea: |
| |
| |
| |
| |
| |

| Date: |
|---|
| Source: |
| Idea: |
|  |
|  |
|  |
|  |
|  |

| Date: |
|---|
| Source: |
| Idea: |
|  |
|  |
|  |
|  |
|  |

| Date: |
|---|
| Source: |
| Idea: |
|  |
|  |
|  |
|  |
|  |

| Date: |
|---|
| Source: |
| Idea: |
| |
| |
| |
| |
| |

| Date: |
|---|
| Source: |
| Idea: |
| |
| |
| |
| |
| |

| Date: |
|---|
| Source: |
| Idea: |
| |
| |
| |
| |
| |

| Date: |
| --- |
| Source: |
| Idea: |
| |
| |
| |
| |
| |

| Date: |
| --- |
| Source: |
| Idea: |
| |
| |
| |
| |
| |

| Date: |
| --- |
| Source: |
| Idea: |
| |
| |
| |
| |
| |

| Date: |
|---|
| Source: |
| Idea: |
|  |
|  |
|  |
|  |
|  |

| Date: |
|---|
| Source: |
| Idea: |
|  |
|  |
|  |
|  |
|  |

| Date: |
|---|
| Source: |
| Idea: |
|  |
|  |
|  |
|  |
|  |

Date:

Source:

Idea:

---

Date:

Source:

Idea:

---

Date:

Source:

Idea:

| Date: |
| Source: |
| Idea: |
| |
| |
| |
| |
| |

| Date: |
| Source: |
| Idea: |
| |
| |
| |
| |
| |

| Date: |
| Source: |
| Idea: |
| |
| |
| |
| |
| |

| Date: |
|---|
| Source: |
| Idea: |
| |
| |
| |
| |
| |

| Date: |
|---|
| Source: |
| Idea: |
| |
| |
| |
| |
| |

| Date: |
|---|
| Source: |
| Idea: |
| |
| |
| |
| |
| |

| Date: |
| --- |
| Source: |
| Idea: |
| |
| |
| |
| |
| |

| Date: |
| --- |
| Source: |
| Idea: |
| |
| |
| |
| |
| |

| Date: |
| --- |
| Source: |
| Idea: |
| |
| |
| |
| |
| |

| Date: |
|---|
| Source: |
| Idea: |
| |
| |
| |
| |
| |

| Date: |
|---|
| Source: |
| Idea: |
| |
| |
| |
| |
| |

| Date: |
|---|
| Source: |
| Idea: |
| |
| |
| |
| |
| |

| Date: |
| --- |
| Source: |
| Idea: |
|  |
|  |
|  |
|  |
|  |

| Date: |
| --- |
| Source: |
| Idea: |
|  |
|  |
|  |
|  |
|  |

| Date: |
| --- |
| Source: |
| Idea: |
|  |
|  |
|  |
|  |
|  |

| Date: |
|---|
| Source: |
| Idea: |
|  |
|  |
|  |
|  |
|  |

| Date: |
|---|
| Source: |
| Idea: |
|  |
|  |
|  |
|  |
|  |

| Date: |
|---|
| Source: |
| Idea: |
|  |
|  |
|  |
|  |
|  |

| Date: |
|---|
| Source: |
| Idea: |
| |
| |
| |
| |
| |

| Date: |
|---|
| Source: |
| Idea: |
| |
| |
| |
| |
| |

| Date: |
|---|
| Source: |
| Idea: |
| |
| |
| |
| |
| |

| Date: |
| Source: |
| Idea: |
| |
| |
| |
| |
| |

| Date: |
| Source: |
| Idea: |
| |
| |
| |
| |
| |

| Date: |
| Source: |
| Idea: |
| |
| |
| |
| |
| |

| Date: |
|---|
| Source: |
| Idea: |
| |
| |
| |
| |
| |

| Date: |
|---|
| Source: |
| Idea: |
| |
| |
| |
| |
| |

| Date: |
|---|
| Source: |
| Idea: |
| |
| |
| |
| |
| |

| Date: |
| Source: |
| Idea: |
| |
| |
| |
| |
| |
| |

| Date: |
| Source: |
| Idea: |
| |
| |
| |
| |
| |
| |

| Date: |
| Source: |
| Idea: |
| |
| |
| |
| |
| |
| |

| Date: |
| Source: |
| Idea: |
| |
| |
| |
| |
| |

| Date: |
| Source: |
| Idea: |
| |
| |
| |
| |
| |

| Date: |
| Source: |
| Idea: |
| |
| |
| |
| |
| |

| Date: |
| Source: |
| Idea: |
| |
| |
| |
| |
| |

| Date: |
| Source: |
| Idea: |
| |
| |
| |
| |
| |

| Date: |
| Source: |
| Idea: |
| |
| |
| |
| |
| |

| Date: |
| --- |
| Source: |
| Idea: |
| |
| |
| |
| |
| |

| Date: |
| --- |
| Source: |
| Idea: |
| |
| |
| |
| |
| |

| Date: |
| --- |
| Source: |
| Idea: |
| |
| |
| |
| |
| |

| Date: |
|---|
| Source: |
| Idea: |
| |
| |
| |
| |
| |

| Date: |
|---|
| Source: |
| Idea: |
| |
| |
| |
| |
| |

| Date: |
|---|
| Source: |
| Idea: |
| |
| |
| |
| |
| |

| Date: |
| :--- |
| Source: |
| Idea: |
| |
| |
| |
| |
| |

| Date: |
| :--- |
| Source: |
| Idea: |
| |
| |
| |
| |
| |

| Date: |
| :--- |
| Source: |
| Idea: |
| |
| |
| |
| |
| |

| Date: |
|---|
| Source: |
| Idea: |
| |
| |
| |
| |
| |

| Date: |
|---|
| Source: |
| Idea: |
| |
| |
| |
| |
| |

| Date: |
|---|
| Source: |
| Idea: |
| |
| |
| |
| |
| |

| Date: |
| Source: |
| Idea: |
| |
| |
| |
| |
| |

| Date: |
| Source: |
| Idea: |
| |
| |
| |
| |
| |

| Date: |
| Source: |
| Idea: |
| |
| |
| |
| |
| |

Date:

Source:

Idea:

---

Date:

Source:

Idea:

---

Date:

Source:

Idea:

| Date: |
| Source: |
| Idea: |
| |
| |
| |
| |
| |

| Date: |
| Source: |
| Idea: |
| |
| |
| |
| |
| |

| Date: |
| Source: |
| Idea: |
| |
| |
| |
| |
| |

| Date: |
| Source: |
| Idea: |
| |
| |
| |
| |
| |

| Date: |
| Source: |
| Idea: |
| |
| |
| |
| |
| |

| Date: |
| Source: |
| Idea: |
| |
| |
| |
| |
| |

| Date: |
| --- |
| Source: |
| Idea: |
|  |
|  |
|  |
|  |
|  |

| Date: |
| --- |
| Source: |
| Idea: |
|  |
|  |
|  |
|  |
|  |

| Date: |
| --- |
| Source: |
| Idea: |
|  |
|  |
|  |
|  |
|  |

| Date: |
|---|
| Source: |
| Idea: |
| |
| |
| |
| |
| |

| Date: |
|---|
| Source: |
| Idea: |
| |
| |
| |
| |
| |

| Date: |
|---|
| Source: |
| Idea: |
| |
| |
| |
| |
| |

| Date: |
| Source: |
| Idea: |
| |
| |
| |
| |
| |

| Date: |
| Source: |
| Idea: |
| |
| |
| |
| |
| |

| Date: |
| Source: |
| Idea: |
| |
| |
| |
| |
| |

| Date: |
|---|
| Source: |
| Idea: |
| |
| |
| |
| |
| |
| |

| Date: |
|---|
| Source: |
| Idea: |
| |
| |
| |
| |
| |
| |

| Date: |
|---|
| Source: |
| Idea: |
| |
| |
| |
| |
| |
| |

| Date: |
| Source: |
| Idea: |
| |
| |
| |
| |
| |

| Date: |
| Source: |
| Idea: |
| |
| |
| |
| |
| |

| Date: |
| Source: |
| Idea: |
| |
| |
| |
| |
| |

| Date: |
| Source: |
| Idea: |
| |
| |
| |
| |
| |

| Date: |
| Source: |
| Idea: |
| |
| |
| |
| |
| |

| Date: |
| Source: |
| Idea: |
| |
| |
| |
| |
| |

| Date: |
|---|
| Source: |
| Idea: |
|  |
|  |
|  |
|  |
|  |

| Date: |
|---|
| Source: |
| Idea: |
|  |
|  |
|  |
|  |
|  |

| Date: |
|---|
| Source: |
| Idea: |
|  |
|  |
|  |
|  |
|  |

| Date: |
|---|
| Source: |
| Idea: |
| |
| |
| |
| |
| |

| Date: |
|---|
| Source: |
| Idea: |
| |
| |
| |
| |
| |

| Date: |
|---|
| Source: |
| Idea: |
| |
| |
| |
| |
| |

| Date: |
| Source: |
| Idea: |
| |
| |
| |
| |
| |

| Date: |
| Source: |
| Idea: |
| |
| |
| |
| |
| |

| Date: |
| Source: |
| Idea: |
| |
| |
| |
| |
| |

| Date: |
| Source: |
| Idea: |
|  |
|  |
|  |
|  |
|  |

| Date: |
| Source: |
| Idea: |
|  |
|  |
|  |
|  |
|  |

| Date: |
| Source: |
| Idea: |
|  |
|  |
|  |
|  |
|  |

| Date: |
|---|
| Source: |
| Idea: |
| |
| |
| |
| |
| |

| Date: |
|---|
| Source: |
| Idea: |
| |
| |
| |
| |
| |

| Date: |
|---|
| Source: |
| Idea: |
| |
| |
| |
| |
| |

| Date: |
| Source: |
| Idea: |
| |
| |
| |
| |
| |

| Date: |
| Source: |
| Idea: |
| |
| |
| |
| |
| |

| Date: |
| Source: |
| Idea: |
| |
| |
| |
| |
| |

| Date: |
|---|
| Source: |
| Idea: |
| |
| |
| |
| |
| |

| Date: |
|---|
| Source: |
| Idea: |
| |
| |
| |
| |
| |

| Date: |
|---|
| Source: |
| Idea: |
| |
| |
| |
| |
| |

Date:

Source:

Idea:

---

Date:

Source:

Idea:

---

Date:

Source:

Idea:

| Date:   |
|---------|
| Source: |
| Idea:   |
|         |
|         |
|         |
|         |
|         |

| Date:   |
|---------|
| Source: |
| Idea:   |
|         |
|         |
|         |
|         |
|         |

| Date:   |
|---------|
| Source: |
| Idea:   |
|         |
|         |
|         |
|         |
|         |

| Date: |
|---|
| Source: |
| Idea: |
| |
| |
| |
| |
| |

| Date: |
|---|
| Source: |
| Idea: |
| |
| |
| |
| |
| |

| Date: |
|---|
| Source: |
| Idea: |
| |
| |
| |
| |
| |

| Date: |
| :--- |
| Source: |
| Idea: |
| |
| |
| |
| |
| |

| Date: |
| :--- |
| Source: |
| Idea: |
| |
| |
| |
| |
| |

| Date: |
| :--- |
| Source: |
| Idea: |
| |
| |
| |
| |
| |

| Date: |
| Source: |
| Idea: |
| |
| |
| |
| |
| |

| Date: |
| Source: |
| Idea: |
| |
| |
| |
| |
| |

| Date: |
| Source: |
| Idea: |
| |
| |
| |
| |
| |

| Date: |
| --- |
| Source: |
| Idea: |
|  |
|  |
|  |
|  |
|  |

| Date: |
| --- |
| Source: |
| Idea: |
|  |
|  |
|  |
|  |
|  |

| Date: |
| --- |
| Source: |
| Idea: |
|  |
|  |
|  |
|  |
|  |

| Date: |
| :--- |
| Source: |
| Idea: |
| |
| |
| |
| |
| |
| |

| Date: |
| :--- |
| Source: |
| Idea: |
| |
| |
| |
| |
| |
| |

| Date: |
| :--- |
| Source: |
| Idea: |
| |
| |
| |
| |
| |
| |

| Date:   |
|---------|
| Source: |
| Idea:   |
|         |
|         |
|         |
|         |
|         |

| Date:   |
|---------|
| Source: |
| Idea:   |
|         |
|         |
|         |
|         |
|         |

| Date:   |
|---------|
| Source: |
| Idea:   |
|         |
|         |
|         |
|         |
|         |

| Date: |
|-------|
| Source: |
| Idea: |
| |
| |
| |
| |
| |

| Date: |
|-------|
| Source: |
| Idea: |
| |
| |
| |
| |
| |

| Date: |
|-------|
| Source: |
| Idea: |
| |
| |
| |
| |
| |

| Date: |
|---|
| Source: |
| Idea: |
| |
| |
| |
| |
| |

| Date: |
|---|
| Source: |
| Idea: |
| |
| |
| |
| |
| |

| Date: |
|---|
| Source: |
| Idea: |
| |
| |
| |
| |
| |

| Date: |
|---|
| Source: |
| Idea: |
| |
| |
| |
| |
| |

| Date: |
|---|
| Source: |
| Idea: |
| |
| |
| |
| |
| |

| Date: |
|---|
| Source: |
| Idea: |
| |
| |
| |
| |
| |

| Date: |
| --- |
| Source: |
| Idea: |
| |
| |
| |
| |
| |

| Date: |
| --- |
| Source: |
| Idea: |
| |
| |
| |
| |
| |

| Date: |
| --- |
| Source: |
| Idea: |
| |
| |
| |
| |
| |

Date:

Source:

Idea:

---

Date:

Source:

Idea:

---

Date:

Source:

Idea:

| Date: |
|---|
| Source: |
| Idea: |
| |
| |
| |
| |
| |

| Date: |
|---|
| Source: |
| Idea: |
| |
| |
| |
| |
| |

| Date: |
|---|
| Source: |
| Idea: |
| |
| |
| |
| |
| |

| Date: |
| Source: |
| Idea: |
| |
| |
| |
| |
| |

| Date: |
| Source: |
| Idea: |
| |
| |
| |
| |
| |

| Date: |
| Source: |
| Idea: |
| |
| |
| |
| |
| |

| Date: |
|---|
| Source: |
| Idea: |
| |
| |
| |
| |

| Date: |
|---|
| Source: |
| Idea: |
| |
| |
| |
| |

| Date: |
|---|
| Source: |
| Idea: |
| |
| |
| |
| |

| Date: |
|---|
| Source: |
| Idea: |
| |
| |
| |
| |
| |

| Date: |
|---|
| Source: |
| Idea: |
| |
| |
| |
| |
| |

| Date: |
|---|
| Source: |
| Idea: |
| |
| |
| |
| |
| |

| Date: |
| Source: |
| Idea: |
|  |
|  |
|  |
|  |
|  |

| Date: |
| Source: |
| Idea: |
|  |
|  |
|  |
|  |
|  |

| Date: |
| Source: |
| Idea: |
|  |
|  |
|  |
|  |
|  |

| Date: |
|---|
| Source: |
| Idea: |
| |
| |
| |
| |
| |

| Date: |
|---|
| Source: |
| Idea: |
| |
| |
| |
| |
| |

| Date: |
|---|
| Source: |
| Idea: |
| |
| |
| |
| |
| |

| Date: |
| Source: |
| Idea: |
| |
| |
| |
| |
| |

| Date: |
| Source: |
| Idea: |
| |
| |
| |
| |
| |

| Date: |
| Source: |
| Idea: |
| |
| |
| |
| |
| |

| Date: |
|---|
| Source: |
| Idea: |
|  |
|  |
|  |
|  |
|  |

| Date: |
|---|
| Source: |
| Idea: |
|  |
|  |
|  |
|  |
|  |

| Date: |
|---|
| Source: |
| Idea: |
|  |
|  |
|  |
|  |
|  |

| Date: |
|---|
| Source: |
| Idea: |
| |
| |
| |
| |
| |

| Date: |
|---|
| Source: |
| Idea: |
| |
| |
| |
| |
| |

| Date: |
|---|
| Source: |
| Idea: |
| |
| |
| |
| |
| |

| Date: |
|---|
| Source: |
| Idea: |
| |
| |
| |
| |
| |

# *About the Author*

---------- ◆ ----------

**Tim McMahon** is one of today's leading speakers on strategies for personal and business success. Besides keynoting major conferences and events around the world, Tim actively works with client companies on Value

Selling, business process re-engineering and the application of CRM and e-business technologies as tools for new competitive advantage.

At the national *Sales Management Conference*, Tim was recognized as *"one of the world's top three gurus in sales and management"* *(Timothy McMahon, Tom Peters, and Al Reis)*.

A veteran sales representative and sales manager, Tim spent over twenty years with IBM, Digital Equipment, and Dun+Bradstreet corporations in sales and senior management positions.

McMahon is the author of three books, *Selling 2000, Solving the Sales Manager Equation*, and *Dear God! I Never Wanted to Be a Salesman!* and is the publisher of *"The Value Proposition"* magazine. He wrote the syndicated column *McMahon On Management*, and recently completed a special for *The Computer Channel* on "Selling & Technology in the 21st Century Sales Organization".

He holds a B.A. degree from Indiana University, and is currently a doctoral candidate in management. He also served in the United States Marine Corps.

Tim McMahon and his family reside in New Hampshire.

For more information, visit Tim's website at:

www.mcmahonworldwide.com

www.ingramcontent.com/pod-product-compliance
Lightning Source LLC
Chambersburg PA
CBHW030801180526
45163CB00003B/1114